Ethereum
Master the Ether and Profit the Opportunity

David Chang

Copyright © 2017 David Chang

All rights reserved.

The follow eBook is reproduced below with the goal of providing information that is as accurate and reliable as possible. Regardless, purchasing this eBook can be seen as consent to the fact that both the publisher and the author of this book are in no way experts on the topics discussed within and that any recommendations or suggestions that are made herein are for entertainment purposes only. Professionals should be consulted as needed prior to undertaking any of the action endorsed herein.

This declaration is deemed fair and valid by both the American Bar Association and the Committee of Publishers Association

Furthermore, the transmission, duplication or reproduction of any of the following work including specific information will be considered an illegal act irrespective of if it is done electronically or in print. This extends to creating a secondary or tertiary copy of the work or a recorded copy and is only allowed with express written consent from the Publisher. All additional right reserved.

The information in the following pages is broadly considered to be a truthful and accurate account of facts and as such any inattention, use or misuse of the information in question by the reader will render any resulting actions solely under their purview. There are no scenarios in which the publisher or the original author of this work can be in any fashion deemed liable for any hardship or damages that may befall them after undertaking information described herein.

Additionally, the information in the following pages is intended only for informational purposes and should thus be thought of as universal. As befitting its nature, it is presented without assurance regarding its prolonged validity or interim quality. Trademarks that are mentioned are done without written consent and can in no way be considered an endorsement from the trademark holder.

ISBN-13:978-1979834414
ISBN-10:1979834415

CONTENTS

Ethereum: The Network	1
What is Ether?	33
Opportunity in Ethereum	55
Conclusion	79

INTRODUCTION

If you have spent much time browsing through the Internet, you have probably stumbled across something related to Ethereum. It may be the idea of blockchain technology, a Dapp (decentralized application), the value of the Ether or predictions regarding its future activity, mining, or the social movement of decentralization. Something may have piqued your interest, and you want to know more. You have searched for information, but articles and videos on Ethereum are largely obtuse and filled with heady information more appropriate for computer geeks than for someone with an amateurish interest. Still, your interest has grown. You have learned that the Ether is a cryptocurrency that has been increasing in value at rates never before seen in the history of finance. You have learned that Ethereum is a network built on blockchain technology, and that its Dapps are run entirely automatically. Maybe you have even used some Dapps or otherwise performed transactions on Ethereum. Maybe you have even bought Ether.

And you want to know even more. Congratulations on finding this book, which will help you further explore and understand the Ethereum phenomenon. This book assumes that you already have some basic knowledge about Ethereum, but still breaks down some of the more difficult concepts into layman's terms. It's not for computer geeks but for average people who want to become a part of the Ethereum movement. If that person is you, read on. Inside, you'll find information on what blockchain technology is and how the mechanics behind it work. You'll learn about the Ethereum Virtual Machine, mining, gas and the internal pricing of Ethereum, the history of the network, and more. You'll even learn some ways that you can make money on Ethereum, either by building a Dapp, using a Dapp, or investing in Ether.

Keep reading to find out more!

ETHEREUM: THE NETWORK

Blockchain

In order to understand Ethereum and how it works, you first need to understand some of the basics behind the technology used to build the network. Vitalik Buterin, the Russian-Canadian young man who developed Ethereum, worked extensively with the Bitcoin community. Bitcoin runs on a new type of technology called blockchain. Buterin realized the huge potential that blockchain had, which wasn't being utilized by Bitcoin. He decided to leave the Bitcoin community in order to capitalize on the potentials of blockchain by creating Ethereum.

Blockchain was created by an anonymous individual known only as Satoshi Nakamoto. Nakamoto set out to create a digital currency that would not have the problem of double spending. Double spending refers to spending the same amount of currency twice. For example, imagine that you have $50 in your bank account, and you owe both Jack and Jill $50 each. You write both of them a check for $50, knowing that only one of them will be able to cash it. Whoever gets to the bank first will get to cash the check; the other one will be left without the money owed.

While in the world of traditional finance and banking the person, who didn't make it to the bank first would be able to find a way to get paid, the problem gets a bit more complicated when you are dealing exclusively with the digital world and no centralized institution running the show. Imagine that you have $50 that exists only in a digital format and is not held by a central bank. Theoretically, you could set up online payments to both Jack and Jill and press "send" at almost the exact same time. Before one payment could be processed, both would be completed. You successfully spent that same $50 two times.

Nakamoto wanted to find a way to avoid this problem. The solution was blockchain. The next few sections will explain some of the mechanics behind blockchain — what it does and how it works.

The Traditional Client/Server Model

Most computer programs run on a

traditional model known as the client/server model. Say that you want to do some online shopping for a new bed set. You log on to your account at the shopping website and are then able to peruse through all of the merchandise available for you to buy. You select a new bedspread, warm blanket, and sheets, add them to your cart, and submit the purchase. Easy enough, right?

Behind the scenes, a lot more is going on. When you log in, your computer becomes a client of the online shopping company's main server. This main server houses all of the company's data and information, including your personal information — such as your credit card number and address —

stored on your account. If something were to happen to that main server, at best the entire network would go down, and at worst your personal information would be compromised.

Say that a hacker is able to break into the main server from the comfort of his mom's basement. He injects a virus into the source code that runs the website, effectively shutting it down. That order that you just made and paid for is now completely scrambled, and there is no record of the items that you purchased. While the website is down and technicians are scrambling to fix the problem, he is able to siphon off your credit card number and address and coolly walk away with your finances.

This is not just a hypothetical scenario. Hacks like this routinely occur in banks, credit card companies, and commercial stores.

There seems to be an easy solution for the company: implement cybersecurity features that prevent hackers from being able to break into the main server. However, cybersecurity is, at best, only able to stay half a step ahead of hackers. They are constantly coming up with new ways to override any new security measures. Major companies spend millions of dollars every year on cybersecurity, turning it into a multi-billion-dollar industry. And yet, the problem of hacking remains.

Blockchain's Peer-to-Peer Model

In the late 1990s and early 2000s, a cybersecurity specialist out of Cambridge University named Ross Anderson published some papers highlighting the problems of the traditional client/server model. He proposed that what was needed was not tighter cybersecurity but rather a complete paradigm shift in the way that networks operate.

On October 31, 2008, Satoshi Nakamoto released a white paper for a peer-to-peer currency that he called Bitcoin. The white paper described an entirely new programming system on which Bitcoin would run; he called it blockchain. Blockchain would solve both the security problems and eliminate the possibility of double spending.

Instead of all of the data being stored in a central server, Nakamoto's design called for a series of computers, referred to as nodes, through which the information would pass. Each node would be operated by an individual who was part of the network, and the information would have to pass through the nodes rather than through a central server. This created a new type of network, a peer-to-peer network.

With a peer-to-peer network, there is no central server for a hacker to break into. In order for the network to become compromised, 51 percent of those who operate a node would have to be in collusion with the hacker and agree to manipulate the data. Additionally, because all of the information has to pass through each of the nodes, it is visible to everyone, although the names of people involved in transactions are kept anonymous. This feature creates a high degree of accountability; if there is a problem anywhere on the blockchain, everyone in the network will know immediately.

A Digital Ledger

So, how does this fix the problem of double spending? A deeper look into how blockchain works will reveal how it solved this problem.

Blockchain is essentially a digital ledger. A ledger is nothing more than an account of transactions that have occurred. When you log in to your bank account, you are looking at a ledger. It shows all of your deposits, withdrawals, and current balance. Companies keep ledgers, which are usually maintained by accountants. Challenges arise when those ledgers are kept hidden and people behind the scenes are manipulating the data in them. This scenario is what led to the fall of Enron in 2000: Accountants were shifting funds around and making their ledgers appear to show that the company was solvent. By the time the fraud was discovered, millions of people had lost their investments.

Blockchain solves this problem of fraud by maintain all of its data publicly in a digital ledger. All of the information in the ledger is publicly available, so there is no question as to whether or not fraud or other unethical practices are occurring.

Every time a transaction is made on a blockchain, the information from that transaction is stored in a block. When enough transactions have occurred to fill up a block, that block is broadcast to all of the nodes on the network to be verified. Verification occurs through a complex process known as mining, in which the computers solve complex algorithms in order to generate a hash value; this process takes about 10 minutes. Once verified, that hash value is applied to the block. When the next block is presented for verification, the hash value of the previous block is applied to the algorithm in the current block, thereby connecting the two blocks together. The hash value for the new block is generated, and it becomes part of the algorithm for the next block, and so on and so forth. All of these blocks are joined together in a chain, hence the term "blockchain." This technology was designed in order to create the first successful virtual currency, Bitcoin.

Imagine that you use Bitcoin and have 50 Satoshis (a small denomination of a bitcoin). You owe both Jack and Jill 50 Satoshis each, and have cleverly schemed to set up payments to both of them and submit those payments almost simultaneously. If those two transactions end up in the same block, they will both be denied. If they are put into two separate blocks, because the verification process takes a full 10 minutes, one of them will get verified before the other. This means that only either Jack or Jill, not both of them, will get the money owed. The problem of double spending was solved.

All of these features were developed to create Bitcoin, but they will be important in terms of understanding the mechanics behind Ethereum.

The Ethereum Virtual Machine

The Ethereum Virtual Machine is like the world computer of the entire Ethereum network. Every node on the Ethereum network is connected to it, causing it to span the entire globe. It is not a physical computer or piece of hardware, but rather the program behind Ethereum.

A virtual machine is an emulation of a physical computer and provides the same functionality. It can be an application environment or an operating system that runs on a physical computer by being installed on the software. When the file is opened, it runs as if it is a computer separate from the system on which it is installed and running.

Typically, blockchains are open-source programs. This means that the codes that underlie the blockchain are publicly accessible, and people who have the programming knowledge are able to make modifications and improvements to the codes. Those modifications usually must pass through a core programming team for approval before they are implemented in the blockchain as part of its code.

The Ethereum Virtual Machine is a system on which developers can create and execute code on the Ethereum network. It functions somewhat like a sandbox; a sandbox is a program that allows a code to be tested using only minimal resources. If the code is somehow defective, only a small part of the system is harmed.

Programmers are able to use the EVM to develop Dapps, or decentralized applications. Just like finances in the modern world are largely governed by centralized institutions such as banks and governments, internet apps usually run through a centralized institution. For example, if you use Gmail, your email passes through Google as a third person or intermediary. A Dapp is a special type of application that plays on the philosophy behind Bitcoin and the blockchain revolution: decentralization and peer-to-peer network.

A Dapp is not owned by any particular entity but rather is collectively owned by the blockchain. Consider how Twitter works. If someone posts a controversial tweet, that person can either go back and erase it or Twitter may censor it so that it effectively disappears. Imagine that an application like Twitter is run as a Dapp instead of a traditional application. Once the information is entered into a smart contract and is verified, it becomes an immutable part of the entire blockchain. There is no way to go back and change any of the information. In other words, that tweet cannot be deleted, not even by the person who created the Dapp.

In addition to allowing developers to create Dapps, the EVM provides the mechanism for transactions on the Ethereum blockchain to be verified. The EVM is connected to every node on the Ethereum network, so all transactions must pass through it. Since thousands of computers are connected to the EVM, one might expect that it would be incredibly fast and efficient. However, the exact opposite is true. Transactions on the blockchain must be verified by all of the nodes, making the EVM actually much slower than traditional, physical computers. What it lacks in speed and efficiency it makes up for in security, accuracy and the fact that it can be accessed from anywhere in the world.

Turing Completeness. Alan Turing was a British computer scientist who is possibly most famous for breaking the unbreakable German enigma code. He developed a machine that theoretically, given enough time and resources, could solve any computation. That machine became known as the Turing machine and was the foundation of the modern computer.

A Turing complete system is one that, like the original Turing machine, is able to run any type of program. A calculator is a type of computer that is not Turing complete; it can only perform certain mathematical calculations. However, your PC probably is Turing complete because, given enough time and resources, it can run any program.

Bitcoin, the original blockchain, was revolutionary in terms of computer programming and a social movement of decentralization. However, it is not Turing complete because it can only be used to engage in Bitcoin transactions. Like a calculator can only perform mathematical calculations, Bitcoin can only do Bitcoin transactions.

Ethereum, which was inspired by Bitcoin, is Turing complete because it can run any type of program. Like Bitcoin it is used in transfers of cryptocurrency, but it is also used in the creation of Dapps that serve many different purposes. Some Dapps are for betting on esports, some are for microblogging, some are for making market predictions, some are for business improvement, and some even exist to hold charities accountable for the work that they profess to do. The possibilities for Dapps and what they can be programmed to do are endless. Therefore, Ethereum is Turing complete.

So, why does Ethereum allow for the development of Dapps while Bitcoin doesn't? The simple answer is that Bitcoin wasn't designed to. Vitalik Buterin, before creating Ethereum, worked extensively with Bitcoin and realized the huge potential that lay within blockchain technology. However, Bitcoin just wasn't built for that purpose. Buterin went on to design Ethereum as a means for expanding the use of blockchain technology by allowing developers to build Dapps.

History of Ethereum

The history of Ethereum really begins with its creator, Vitalik Buterin. Buterin was born in Kolomna, Russia, a province of Moscow, in 1994. His family emigrated to Canada when he was six because of the opportunities that would be afforded. Buterin quickly showed a high intelligence and uncanny aptitude for mathematics, which he used to begin developing his skills as a computer programmer. When he was 17, his father introduced him to Bitcoin. He began writing for a Bitcoin blog and became an editor of *Bitcoin Magazine* in 2011. He continued working with the Bitcoin community, especially as a writer, and came to realize the profound potential that lay within blockchain technology.

In 2013, Buterin wrote a white paper for Ethereum in which he described what the proposed network would do. The following year, he was awarded a $100,000 grant from the Thiel Fellowship to pursue his idea. He dropped out of the University of Waterloo and devoted himself full-time to the creation of Ethereum. Other developers joined him in building the network. In July 2014, a public crowdsale was made to further fund Ethereum. Digital tokens that would underlie the network, known as ether, were sold to raise money. People who bought the ether at the crowdsale effectively bought shares in the project. Sixty million ether were sold, raising about $18 million.

Ethereum creators began a proof-of-concept series later that year to test the network's viability, including its ability to hold up under a large load of information. The proof-of-concept series began with 0.1 and went through 0.9. 0.9 was known as Olympic and was designed to test the limits of the blockchain. People were actually encouraged to spam the network as much as they could to see how well it was able to bear large amounts of input. People who tested the proof-of-concept series were able to claim ether as a reward.

Ethereum went live on July 30, 2015, in its earliest format, known as Frontier, also known as Ethereum 1.0. Frontier was a bit of a bare-bones version of Ethereum and was meant for developers to be able to contribute to the project. The code for the program had been written, but there was as of yet no blockchain because no transactions had been made. Developers who wanted to join in on the project were able to load what was known as the Genesis block, or the first block in the blockchain. The mining of the Genesis block marked the official beginning of Ethereum.

Frontier was far from a perfect version of Ethereum; developers were notified before downloading the software that there would be issues associated with it, including bugs and updates. In March 2016, Frontier was upgraded to a new version known as Homestead. Homestead was automatically added at block number 1,150,000 in the blockchain. The transition to Homestead required something called a hard fork. A hard fork is a change in the blockchain's protocols that cannot be implemented backward into already existing blocks. It effectively splits the path of a blockchain by not accepting verifications from nodes that do not use the updated version.

A month later, a Dapp known as The

DAO (Decentralized Autonomous Organization) introduced a token sale to crowdfund its upcoming launch. The DAO was a stateless program (not connected to any political or geographical territory) that provided a new business model of decentralization, which could be applied to both commercial and nonprofit businesses. The token sale was a huge success; it became the largest crowdfunding campaign up until that time. People could use ether to buy DAO tokens, which would fuel their access to the DAO. 18,000 people bought nearly 12 million ether worth of DAO tokens, the total value of which came to over $150 million. The DAO seemed to be completely primed for a successful run as a Dapp.

Keep in mind that no one owns a Dapp, or any information on the blockchain, for that matter. The codes are open source, meaning that they are publicly available. Shortly into the crowdfunding campaign, a paper was published that noted some of the security issues and vulnerabilities within the code that could potentially be exploited by an unethical individual. Other programmers noticed the weakness, and some even blogged about it, calling for it to be fixed. On June 17, just a couple of weeks after The DAO went live, an unknown individual attacked the Dapp and siphoned off one-third of its assets.

In response to the attack, the value of the Ether began to tumble, going from about $21.50 to $15 in just a few hours. The creators of Ethereum and of The DAO immediately got to work coming up with a solution to the problem before the Ether depreciated even more and the entire network was called into question. The solution was a controversial one: to instate a hard fork in the network, which would allow investors to get back the ether that they had invested. Some were against the hard fork because it challenged the immutable nature of blockchain technology, potentially introducing a dangerous precedent of censorship. They also felt that returning the ether spent on DAO tokens was the equivalent of a bailout. However, those in favor of the hard fork felt that instead of saying that the code used to create

The DAO was law and unchangeable, they should fall back on the spirit behind peer-to-peer blockchain: the consensus of the people and social parity. Returning the funds was not a bailout but rather an ethical obligation because the users had been robbed. The decision to make the hard fork and handle the situation through social obligations and consensus may have kept the matter from being investigated by courts.

After the hard fork, some users opted to stay on the original version of Ethereum, which became known as Ethereum Classic. These users generally were against the hard fork because it violated the immutability of the blockchain. They insist that the programming code used is law, and if it has problems and deficiencies, the responsibility lies with the people using it. They also believe that the hard fork introduced centralization, something that they are vehemently against. On July 20, 2016, the Ethereum Classic community released its Declaration of Independence, in which it listed some of the Ethereum values that it believed to have been violated. It is no longer considered a standard part of Ethereum, and to symbolize its independence, it uses the abbreviation ETC (Ethereum Classic) rather than ETH (Ethereum). It has its own cryptocurrency now and runs entirely independent of Ethereum.

In February 2017, the trading giant eToro added the Ether to its trading portfolio, showing how quickly Ethereum was growing and how viable the Ether was proving itself to be. By the next month, Ethereum was handling $450 million in transactions each day. It has had to do a couple more hard forks to deal with problems that have arisen, but these have been less controversial as those against the hard forks use Ethereum Classic.

Today, Ethereum is bringing blockchain technology into mainstream business. Organizations like banks and even government bodies are looking at ways that they can use Ethereum to optimize their products and services. In all likelihood, Ethereum will become more popular and ambiguous, and the value of the Ether will continue its climb, as it hits the mainstream.

WHAT IS ETHER?

The Fuel for Ethereum

Currency, in its most basic form, is simply what we use to exchange for things that we want or need. We usually think of currency as money, such as dollars or Euros, which are issued by a centralized bank and authorized by the national government. They are guaranteed by the government, and that guarantee is good as long as the government itself does not fail.

With this understanding of currency in mind, the concept of cryptocurrency is a bit baffling to some. Mainstream economists seem to be chief among the naysayers who point to the impending demise of Bitcoin, the Ether, and other cryptocurrencies. However, these economists seem to be lacking a fundamental understanding of currency and the basic laws of supply and demand.

Modern economic theory is rooted heavily in supply and demand. Put simply, if people demand a certain good or service, its value will increase because they are willing to pay more for it. If there is a small supply of something that a lot of people demand, they will pay more for it. In other words, the value of something is determined by how much of it is available and by how much of it people want. When governments regulate the value of the currencies that they issue, they are circumventing this basic principle. They are falsely attaching a value to money based on policies rather than on supply and demand. Cryptocurrencies, because they are peer-to-peer in nature rather than operated by a central body, can only operate through supply and demand.

Cryptocurrencies are also known as virtual currencies because they exist only in digital form rather than as physical cash that can be carried around. Perhaps they seem less "real" than dollars and cents that can be carried around in a wallet. However, their value is certainly real, as their continued success has shown.

The Ether is the virtual currency associated with the Ethereum network. It is somewhat similar to Bitcoin. Both are decentralized rather than being operated by a bank or government, both run on a peer-to-peer blockchain, and both have rapidly increasing values. There is a crucial difference: Bitcoin, like gold, is not attached to an actual commodity. The Ether is. It is used to power the Ethereum network, so while Bitcoin could theoretically fail if enough users pulled out, the only way for the Ether to fail is for people to stop using Ethereum.

If bitcoins are like gold, think of ether as being like diamonds. Gold's value is not determined by what a central entity says it is worth but by how much people are willing to pay for it. The Disney movie *Pocahontas* gave a meaningful picture of how the value of gold is determined. The English settlers, including John Smith, sailed to the New World in search of gold. John Smith explained to Pocahontas that he was looking for gold; he described it as being yellowish in color and worth a lot. She exclaimed that they have a lot of gold there and produced an ear of corn. Corn has a yellowish color, and in her culture, it was worth a lot. So why was the precious metal known as gold so valuable to John Smith? Because in England, a lot of people wanted it and were willing to pay a lot of money for it. It could be used in jewelry and decoration, thereby showing a person's status. Having gold was a means to show that you were wealthy enough to buy it.

Like gold, diamonds have an incredibly high value because of their rarity and the value that people associate with them. If no one was willing to pay hundreds or even thousands of dollars for a single karat, the value of diamonds would certainly go down. However, diamonds have a function that gold does not have: they can be used industrially. Diamonds are commonly used in saws to make the blades stronger, because no substance on earth is stronger than a diamond. While gold could lose its value if people just stop wanting it, diamonds will only lose their value if people stop needing them for things like saws. While Bitcoin could fail if people stopped using it, the Ether will only fail if people stop needing it.

Mining

New ether is created through a process similar to how new bitcoins are created. When a group of transactions is put into a block and ready to be verified, the data in that block, combined with the hash value from the previous block, is translated into an alphanumeric string called a hash. If one single piece of information in that block is changed, the entire hash will change. Therefore, going back and retroactively changing any of the information in a block is impossible as it will disrupt the entire blockchain. The hash generates a complex mathematical algorithm that must be solved in order for the block to be verified. This provides for something called proof of work. Proof of work is the means by which blockchains are able to ensure that a certain amount of time elapses before the block is verified; this procedure is part of making sure that double spending doesn't happen. As subsequent blocks are mined, they become a part of the blockchain. It is all but impossible to go back and retroactively change any of the information once a block is embedded in the blockchain, making the information contained immutable.

Miners, individuals who use their computer power to solve the complex algorithms required to verify the block, then get to work. The computers generate random guesses, and the user of the computer that randomly guesses the answer is awarded 5 new ether. If another user solves the problem simultaneously, he or she is awarded 3 ether. Therefore, the process of verifying the transactions on the Ethereum network provides the means by which new ether are created. The difficulty of the algorithms is dynamically adjusted so that one complete block is able to be generated every 12 seconds.

Mining, therefore, generates new ether tokens and verifies the transactions that occur on the network. Ethereum absolutely could not run without this function and the miners who carry it out.

Mining ether is one way to make money on the Ethereum network. If you want to get started as a miner, the first thing that you will need is a powerful enough computer and a GPU card. You will need to download the Ethereum mining software, which is free, and connect it to a wallet. You will also want to make sure that you have a source of cheap energy so that the mining is profitable, as it does use a lot of energy. The best form of energy for mining is solar or wind, as this is not only significantly cheaper than traditional fossil fuels but also promotes sustainability of the network. You will probably want to join a mining pool, which will increase your probability of solving the algorithms and getting paid in ether.

Gas

If you want to go somewhere in your car, you have to make sure that you have gas in it. If you have an electric car, you have to make sure that there is enough of a charge to get you to your destination. That is the basic concept behind the idea of gas in Ethereum: in order for your transaction to have the fuel it needs to move forward, you have to have enough gas.

Blockchain networks are huge. They have to be in order for there to be enough people to maintain them. Because there is no centralized authority regulating transactions, there has to be a critical number of people running the peer-to-peer network to ensure that all of the transactions are valid. There are thousands of computers behind the Ethereum world computer; many of them run around the clock and consume large amounts of electricity. In order for mining (the process of validating transactions) to be profitable, miners have to first cover the expenses of running the computers. They have to pay large electricity bills and/or for solar (or another renewable energy source) infrastructure, up-to-date equipment, and hardware, and fans to keep the computers from overheating. The price used to buy gas goes to compensate the miners.

When you go to a gas station to buy gas for your car, the price is fixed; you cannot decide that you want to pay less for gas that may be of a lower quality. On Ethereum, though, you can decide how much to pay for gas. When completing a transaction, you will be shown a sliding scale that registers how much, in Ether, you want to pay for gas. The more you pay, the more incentives that the miners have to validate the block with your transaction. Therefore, paying the higher fee means that your transaction will be processed much faster. If you choose to pay less, miners won't have as much incentive and the block with your transaction will be further down the queue. If you don't buy enough gas, your transaction will face the same dilemma as a car that doesn't have enough: it will stop mid-stream.

The Value of Cryptocurrency

Naysayers and so-called "experts" love to make predictions about the impending doom of the cryptoeconomy.

There have been repeated predictions about the failure of Bitcoin and the Ether, as well as other cryptocurrencies, all of which have been proven false. There is, however, one aspect of the cryptoeconomy that does seem to be particularly troubling for a lot of people, including would-be investors: its extreme volatility. Cryptocurrencies are notorious for having wild fluctuations in their values against the dollar, sometimes losing 25% or more of their value in a single day. Price surges occur as well, with the value skyrocketing so much that economists fear that a bubble is emerging. A bubble occurs when a lot of market speculation occurs; in other words, a value is associated with something that does not have the assets to back up that value. For example, imagine that a fearless and audacious adventurer discovers a new land mass in the middle of the Pacific Ocean. He decides that he wants to capitalize on this discovery by selling portions of it to people who want to move there. He surveys the new island and estimates that it is approximately 35 square miles of rich, fertile, virgin soil and tropical forest. He begins to sell off portions of it in lots and begins to make quite a profit. People rush to buy lots on this island; the value of each lot skyrockets until each one is selling at over a million dollars. Eventually, he sells off all 35 square miles and people begin moving there to take possession of their new land. However, his original estimates were wrong. It is only 20 square miles, the soil is very poor quality, and what he thought were tropical forests were really just big jumbles of thorn bushes. What happened here? People rushed to buy something, paying a lot of money for that actually didn't have much real value at all.

However, cryptocurrencies have proven that they actually do have quite a bit of value, even more so than traditional currencies such as the dollar. They carry a high level of social capital, meaning that they have created a movement among people that goes beyond just finances and all the way to core values that shape both individual lives and a society's ethos: things like distribution of wealth, people being able to make their own monetary policies rather than relying on a central government, and empowering small businesses. These things come back to ideas and values of social justice.

The value of the dollar is largely determined by the US government. Yes, its strength is dependent on how much people are buying, selling, and saving, as well as the balance between imports and exports. However, the government is able to regulate interest rates and create treaties with other countries, all of which can have marked effects on the value of the dollar, effects so strong that the policies enacted by the government effectively determine its value. The values of cryptocurrencies are determined entirely by the people who use them. If a lot of people want to get into the cryptocurrency market, demand is high and the value goes up. The value given is not a false value based on government policies and manipulation, but a true value in the most basic economic sense: it adheres to the immutable and unchangeable laws of supply and demand. Cryptocurrencies are actually a truer, purer form of currency than "traditional" currencies and are *more* economically feasible and stable because they follow basic economic principles.

With the social value of cryptocurrencies in mind, the question emerges of just why they are so volatile. The easy answer is that they are still quite new. The early days of Bitcoin saw incredibly wild value fluctuations, sometimes dropping from the tens of dollars down to a penny and back again within just a few days. Imagine a small puddle made by a recent rainstorm. There isn't much water in it, just like in the early days of Bitcoin, there wasn't much in circulation and weren't many people using it. Now imagine that a 300-pound man does a cannonball into that little puddle. Not only will he probably injure himself, but all of the water in the puddle will be displaced. Similarly, without much cryptocurrency in circulation and not many people using it, just one event was able to disrupt the entire market. One major theft, one political scandal, one piece of mainstream media exposure, just one thing was able to cause the value to plummet or skyrocket.

Now imagine that the same 300-pound man dons a Speedo in preparation for jumping off the high dive into an Olympic-size swimming pool. This pool has vastly larger amounts of water, just like today, there are vastly larger amounts of cryptocurrency in circulation and millions of people using it. Once he goes off the high dive and lands in the water, he will still make a noticeable splash. Major events will have an impact on the cryptocurrency market. However, they won't be catastrophic. The man won't injure himself like he would doing a cannonball into a puddle, and the amount of water displaced will not drain the entire pool. Similarly, while the impact of the events will be felt, they won't drain the entire market or cause the extreme fluctuations seen in the early days of cryptocurrency.

Wild swings still occur. For example, in the summer of 2017, a hoax spread on the Internet claimed that Vitalik Buterin died. The value of the Ether plummeted to a penny. However, as the hoax was revealed to be false, it quickly regained its value.

OPPORTUNITIES IN ETHEREUM

As a public blockchain, Ethereum provides many possibilities and opportunities for earning money. Money earned will usually come either in the form of Ether or as another cryptocurrency on the Ethereum network whose value is tied to the Ether. Opportunities to earn money come in three primary categories: participating in Dapps, building Dapps, and investing in the Ether.

Smart Contracts

Keep in mind that with Bitcoin, data from transactions is stored in a block. In Ethereum, data is stored in something called a smart contract. A smart contract is a trustless agreement between two parties; that agreement will be carried out when certain conditions have been met. There is no need for a third-party intermediary, as the smart contract will automatically fulfill itself.

Imagine that you have health insurance through an insurance company that uses smart contracts to manage policies. The coverage that you pay for and benefits that you are supposed to receive is stored by the smart contract. When you pay your monthly premium, the information from the transaction is stored in the smart contract connected to your policy. Imagine that you develop pneumonia and have to be hospitalized for a week. Based on the coverage information that is stored in the smart contract, the insurance company will automatically release a pre-determined amount of money to cover the cost of your hospital visit. There aren't any phone calls or negotiations involved. No one from the hospital has to haggle with the insurance company, and you don't have to call a lawyer to demand that the insurance company pay what it agreed to pay. Everything was managed by the smart contract.

Imagine that you are on a sports betting website that uses smart contracts, and you have bet the equivalent of $10 that a certain team will win this particular game. Your money is automatically held by the smart contract, so you can't change your mind and decide to bet on the other team instead. When the team you have bet for shows a decisive lead, people who have bet on the other team cannot retroactively change their bets. As soon as the game is over and your team is declared the winner, the money that you are entitled to will automatically be released by the smart contract. This scenario isn't just theoretical; it is actually how an e-sports Ethereum app known as FirstBlood runs.

Ether

So, why do you need ether in order to use Ethereum? Vitalik Buterin developed smart contracts as the basis on which the Ethereum network would run. Smart contracts not only carry out a program's defined parameters but also store the records and other data about a program. In order to execute a smart contract, the terms are sent to every node on the blockchain for verification. Keep in mind that there are a lot of computers on the network, so a lot of energy is expended through the process of mining, which allows the contracts to be verified. In order for miners to be compensated for their work, a certain amount of ether is required to execute the smart contract. This ether is used to pay for gas, which is used to pay the miners.

The need to use ether to pay for gas means that in order to use Ethereum, people have to invest in the Ether. If large-scale corporations, such as major banks, retailers, and even government bodies want to use Ethereum, they will have to buy ether. This means that as the use of smart contracts and demand for Ethereum's abilities increase, so will the value of the Ether. The rise in the Ether's value is not insignificant. In the summer of 2016, it was valued at a paltry $15. A year later, its value had skyrocketed to upwards of $300 and will continue to grow for the foreseeable future.

Bitcoin was a phenomenon in that it turned into a means by which people could unexpectedly become incredibly wealthy. In 2009, a Norwegian man named Kristoffer Koch was writing a thesis on cybersecurity and came across Bitcoin. He invested $27 in it and soon forgot about it. In 2013, he remembered his Bitcoin account and was astounded to find that its value was now $866,000. He used the money to buy an upscale apartment in a wealthy area of Oslo. This case was not an isolated incident, as stories abound of people who invested in Bitcoin and profited immensely from its meteoric rise in value.

The Ether seems to be on the same trajectory as Bitcoin. While its value is still quite volatile and fluctuates on a minute-to-minute basis, it is on an upward climb that shows no sign of slowing down. Economists, journalists, bankers, and politicians repeatedly decry the Ether as being on its way out, just as they routinely do for Bitcoin. However, all of their predictions have proved to be wrong as it continues to soar in value. One way to make money on Ethereum is simply to invest in the Ether. Buy some today so that in the future, maybe just a few short years from now, you can reap the benefits of its increase in value.

There are three ways to invest in the Ether, as with any other currency or traditional investment: short-term holding, long-term holding, and trading. Short-term holding refers to buying some ether (or any other investment) and selling them off when the price goes up. You may decide to hold them for a week or a month or even longer, but you have made the decision that you will sell them to make a profit.

Long-term holding refers to holding your ether for a period of a year or more as a long-term investment. Maybe you are holding on to it in addition to your regular retirement fund or are saving up to buy a home and are relying on the increasing value of the Ether. Maybe you hope to pass it down to your children or grandchildren. Whatever your goal, it is a long-term investment rather than a short-term means of making money.

Trading is the practice of buying when the price drops and selling when the price rises but on an extremely short-term basis. Keep in mind that fluctuations occur on a minute-by-minute basis, so active traders have to be able to act quickly to buy and sell with these rapid fluctuations. Successful traders are able to earn thousands of dollars every week.

Using the Network as a Developer

One way to make money on Ethereum is to develop a Dapp. Keep in mind that there is no guarantee for success; The DAO's success seemed sure, yet a weakness in its code was found and exploited within weeks of going live.

In order to build your own Dapp, first, you need an idea of what you want to do and how it will benefit people. You have to be a visionary with a mindset of furthering the values of transparency and consensus rather than centralization. Consider some of the successful Dapps that are currently in use. FirstBlood, as already mentioned, is a Dapp that brings transparency into the world of esports, which is traditionally fraught with corruption and rigging. In FirstBlood, users make bets on a particular match with a smart contract. The smart contract automatically holds the funds that are bet and releases them once the winner is announced. There is no middleman or referee to authoritatively determine how much money the winners get. The process is entirely automated and transparent, and therefore fraud-free.

Every year, fake charities pop up that exploit and prey on the good intentions of well-meaning people. This happens particularly following major disasters, such as hurricanes and earthquakes. In the midst of a disaster when people are desperate to help in whatever way they can, they may not take the time to search for reputable charities that are on the ground doing relief work. Alice.Si is a Dapp that holds charities accountable for the work that they profess to do. When someone wants to give to a charity via Alice.Si, the money is held in a smart contract and is only released when the charity has met certain objectives. This process ensures that fraudulent charities are not able to access money given through the Dapp.

Bitnation is a virtual country that was inspired by the plight of statelessness. Statelessness is the condition in which one is not a citizen of any country; it was an underlying topic of the movie *The*

Terminal. Examples of stateless people include Kurds, particularly in Turkey; Palestinians; and undocumented immigrants and refugees. Without basic citizenship benefits such as a passport and identifying papers, they are unable to access amenities such as notary and other legal services, travel to other places (even for urgent medical care), and education. Bitnation seeks to change that by allowing people to apply for citizenship to the virtual nation of Bitnation. While the services that it is currently able to provide are quite few, seeing as it is not recognized by any legal entity, it hopes to be able to help end the plight of statelessness.

Augur is a Dapp that makes market predictions based on the consensus of its users. The idea behind it is that when a lot of people provide input as to a particular outcome, as to a small panel of experts, predictions are more likely to occur. This is not only because of their access to information regarding events but because of how they can actually shape the outcome of events. People can log in to Augur and buy into a prediction market for a particular event. That event could be anywhere from what the weather will be like tomorrow, who will win tonight's football game, or who will win an election. If 80% of people on Augur think that Candidate A will win the election, despite what the popular media says, that candidate stands a greater chance of winning. Why? Because the people on Augur are representative of the people who will be voting in the election. People can use the market predictions of Augur to make better decisions because they are more equipped to know what the future will bring.

You can make money on Ethereum by using Dapps like Augur and FirstBlood. However, keep in mind that there is no guarantee that you will make money, and you need to use discretion either when making predictions or placing bets.

Dapps usually run on their own virtual tokens rather than on the Ether. Think of the paradigm like this: When you were a kid and went to an arcade, you probably used your main currency —

dollars — to buy a certain number of tokens, which you could use to play games. The machines at the arcade didn't accept quarters or dollar bills but only tokens that had been provided by the arcade. Using a Dapp is somewhat like going to the arcade before everything became digitized. You exchange a certain amount of ether for a certain number of tokens in order to "play the game." After you have your great idea for what your Dapp will do and how it will benefit the community, you will need to decide what your token will be and how it will work. Will people use it to make bets or predictions? Will they use it to fund charity work? How your token will be used will depend on the nature of your Dapp and what your goals are.

Now that you have a plan laid out for what your Dapp will look like and how its tokens will be used, you need to do the hard work of making a solid plan for how you will build it. This will come in two parts: a programming plan for how you will build and execute the code, and a business plan for how you will fund and implement the Dapp so that it meets its objectives.

First, the programming. You will need to decide which programming language you want to use to build the code and ensure that that is the best one for the job. Maybe you are skilled in C++, but Java is more appropriate for what you want to do. In that case, you may want to find someone who is skilled in Java programming to partner with you. Keep in mind that everything on Ethereum is open source, so your code will be publicly visible. If there is any weakness or deficiency in the code, you can be guaranteed that some unscrupulous individual will find that weakness and bankrupt your Dapp, just like what happened to the DAO. Once you have written the code, you need to apply it to one of the Ethereum mainframes, either Truffle or Embark. Which one you decide to use will depend on your Dapp and what your goals are. After your code is finished, you will need to test it out using the EVM as a sandbox. This will protect your computer and all of the computers on the Ethereum network in case there is something malignant or otherwise unwanted in the code. Once you are satisfied with how the program is running, you will probably want to find some technophile friends to test it out for you. Ask them to look for weaknesses and anyway that funds could be siphoned off. Once you are certain that your code is satisfactory and ready to go, you need to look at the business aspect of launching your Dapp.

Dapps are not free. They cost money to execute, which is usually paid for in gas. The mechanism of gas helps ensure that codes are written as efficiently as possible so that the programs cost less to run. Think of the Dapp that you are creating as if it is a business. You probably won't have employees, seeing as Dapps are designed to be entirely automated and decentralized. However, it is a means of making money by offering some kind of a service to clients. As such, you need a business plan.

Before you get too far, you will want to get input from the Ethereum community. Talk to people who have created successful Dapps. Particularly, look for Dapps whose ambitions are somewhat similar to yours. Find out how people were able to make their Dapps successful. Learn about all of the ins and outs involved in creating a Dapp. In the process, you will be building community support, an invaluable resource as you move down the process of preparing your Dapp for its launch.

Many Dapps crowdfund their initial expenses through something called an Initial Coin Offering, or ICO. An ICO is a campaign in which the public can buy "shares" of a Dapp in the form of digital cryptocurrency tokens. For example, before Ethereum went live, it launched an ICO in which the public was able to buy Ether in the anticipation that its value would increase. The DAO raised close to $200 million in its ICO before it launched. You may want to consider hosting an ICO to raise money and get people interested in your Dapp.

Additionally, you may want to talk to a business analyst who specializes in blockchain about how your Dapp will run financially so that it can remain solvent. You may decide to charge users a membership fee or charge them for the services that they obtain. You may decide to place ads on it so that expenses are covered without having to charge any fees.

Once your business plan is ready and your program is error-free, you are ready to launch your Dapp. Best of luck

CONCLUSION

In conclusion, Ethereum is revolutionizing many aspects of today's digital world. It introduced a new cryptocurrency, the Ether, to rival Bitcoin by not only providing a peer-to-peer medium of exchange but by tying that currency to a particular commodity that people demand: the Ethereum network. Rather than just a currency, Ethereum provides a whole array of Dapps that fundamentally adhere to the philosophies behind the blockchain revolution spawned by Bitcoin. Those philosophies include decentralizing, putting power back into the hands of people, and promoting social justice.

Ethereum has provided new ways of making money, including passive income, that were previously unavailable. People with the computing power and other necessary resources can mine blocks and earn ether as a reward. People can buy into Dapps like Augur and FirstBlood and make money by placing good bets or making correct predictions of future events. People can buy ether tokens, whose value is soaring, and take advantage of the increasing value. They can even build their own Dapps and generate income as if they are running a small business.

Smart contracts are continuing to change aspects of daily life, as mainstream industries are beginning to use them. They hold potential with everything from insurance companies to government institutions such as voting. Because they eliminate all possibility of fraud as well as the need for a middleman, they are cheaper and more efficient to use than other, more traditional methods.

In all likelihood, Ethereum will continue to grow. It will probably experience more hard forks and have other obstacles to overcome, but it has the benefit of the social capital behind the movement that it is a part of.

www.ingramcontent.com/pod-product-compliance
Lightning Source LLC
Chambersburg PA
CBHW070311230526
45470CB00002B/824